Make Me Laugh!

Let the Fun Begin

WACKY WHAT-DO-YOU-GET JOKES, PLAYFUL PUNS, AND MORE

By Scott K. Peterson with Rick and Ann
Walton, Diane and Clint Burns, Larry Adler,
and Peter and Connie Roop
pictures by Brian Gable

Carolrhoda Books, Inc. • Minneapolis

Q: What do you get when you cross King Arthur with a watch?

A: Knight-time.

Q: Why are bananas so attractive?

A: They have plenty of a-peel.

Q: What do lamps wear on sunny days?

A: Their shades.

Q: How do fish practice their music?

A: With scales.

Q: What do you get when you cross Lassie with a rose?

A: A collie-flower.

Q: What would you call a telephone with feet?

A: A walkie-talkie.

Q: What food is never hot?

A: Chili.

Q: Why did the director bring a baseball to the concert?

A: She wanted to have the right pitch.

Q: Why aren't lemons allowed to play music?

A: They make too many sour notes.

Q: Where is the best place to eat along the highway?

A: Wherever there's a fork in the road.

Q: When is a potato like a bad idea?

A: When it's half-baked.

Q: Which president daydreamed?

A: George Wishing-ton.

Q: How does a radio count to ten?

A: 1, 2, 3, 4, 5, 6, 7, 8, 9, antenna.

Q: What do you get when you cross Tom Thumb with Prince Charming?

A: Thumb-prince.

Q: Did you hear about the woman who lost her job as a window washer?

A: She couldn't stand the pane.

Q: Why was the bass singer kicked out of music class?

A: Because he was always getting into treble.

Q: How can you tell when a sewing machine is laughing?

A: Because it's in stitches.

Q: What do people sing underground?

A: Miner scales.

Q: What do you get when you cross candy with matches?

A: A bon-bonfire.

Q: Did you hear about the man who lost his job in the yardstick factory?

A: He bent the rules.

Q: What did the caveman have for lunch?

A: A club sandwich!

Q: What does a lightbulb do with a punching bag?

A: It likes to socket.

Q: Which president liked to cook?

A: Thomas Chef-ferson.

Q: Why is it so easy to talk to a pencil sharpener?

A: Because they get right to the point.

Q: Did you hear about the woman who lost her job as a trapeze artist?

A: She didn't catch on.

Q: How do singers buy things?

A: With har-money.

Q: Who were the smallest presidents?

A: John Atoms and John Quincy Atoms.

Q: Why don't doorbells go to college?

A: Because they're ding-dongs.

Q: What do you get when you cross a beach with your eyes?

A: A see-shore.

Q: What kind of singers do you find at Yellowstone Park?

A: Bear-itones.

Q: What do you get when you cross a bank with a skunk?

A: Dollars and scents.

Fred: Did you hear about the boy who died from eating fifty pancakes?

Ted: How waffle!

Q: What do you get when you cross a river with a bicycle?

A: Wet.

Q: What do you get when you cross a seashell with an electric eel?

A: Shellshock.

Q: Why did the TV set start shaving?

A: Because its picture was getting fuzzy.

Q: Why did the fiddler walk so strangely?

A: Because he was bowlegged.

Q: Why did the baker stop making doughnuts?

A: He got tired of the hole business.

Q: Did you hear about the man who lost his job in the laundromat?

A: He was all washed up.

Pat: Joe the butcher tells such funny jokes!

Nat: Yeah, he's a real cutup!

Q: What's a vacuum cleaner's favorite sport?

A: Rugby.

Q: Did you hear about the woman who lost her job in the picture frame factory?

A: She didn't get the hang of it.

Q: Why did the vacuum cleaner learn self-defense?

A: It was tired of being pushed around.

Q: Did you hear about the woman who lost her job making jigsaw puzzles?

A: She went to pieces.

Q: What kind of sound does a golf cart make?

A: Putt, putt, putt.

Q: What's a vacuum cleaner's favorite candy?

A: A sucker.

Q: Did you hear about the man who lost his job in the weapons factory?

A: He blew up.

Q: Why don't you ever see radios reading books?

A: They're always too busy playing.

Q: What's a lazy person's favorite food?

A: Meat loaf.

Q: What instruments do skeletons like to play?

A: Trombones.

Q: Why shouldn't you take advice from furnaces?

A: Because they just blow hot air.

Q: What do musicians use to brush their teeth?

A: A tuba toothpaste.

Q: What seven letters did the girl say when she opened the refrigerator?

A: "O-I-C-U-R-M-T."

Q: What dance is the president's favorite?

A: The James K. Polk-a.

Mother: Jason, why are you eating hay?

Jason: You always say I eat like a horse!

Q: What do you get when you cross a pig with a bathtub?

A: Hogwash.

Q: Did you hear about the man who lost his job in the perfume factory?

A: He made a big stink.

Q: What do you get when you cross an owl with a duck?

A: A wisequack.

Q: What do you get when you cross a clown with a skeleton?

A: A funnybone.

Q: Why didn't the drummer eat her carrots?

A: Because she liked her beats better.

Q: What do you get when you cross a turkey with slime?

A: Gobbledygook.

Q: Which president made his own clothes?

A: Zachary Taylor.

Q: Which president's favorite holiday was Halloween?

A: James Boo-chanan.

Q: What happened to the drummer who bumped his head?

A: He got a percussion.

Q: Did you hear about the man who lost his job in the coffee factory?

A: He spilled the beans.

Q: What do you get when you cross bubble gum with a raindrop?

A: A gumdrop.

Q: How do you keep two electric frying pans from arguing with each other?

A: Tell them to simmer down.

Q: What do you get when you cross a discount store with a ship?

A: A sale-boat.

Bill: Can you cook an egg in your pajamas?

Will: Yes, but it's easier to use a pan!

Q: Why did the drums fall asleep?

A: Because they were beat.

Q: When a motorboat gets sick, where does it go?

A: To the doc.

Q: What's a bee's favorite song?

A: "I'm Stinging in the Rain."

Q: Why did the baseball coach put an electric mixer in his lineup?

A: He thought it would make a good batter.

Q: What do you do if your coffeemaker is depressed?

A: Try to perk it up.

Q: What did one strawberry say to the other?

A: "You've got to help me. I'm in a jam."

Q: What do you get when you cross a street with your feet?

A: To the other side.

Q: What do you get when you cross a clam with Scrooge?

A: A shellfish person.

Q: Who was the sharpest president?

A: Franklin Pierce.

Q: What do you get when you cross your head with the ocean?

A: Brainwaves.

Q: What's a bully's favorite drink?

A: Punch.

Q: How do piano players eat?

A: With tuning forks.

Q: What do you get when you cross the sun with the ocean?

A: A heat wave.

Q: What did one potato chip say to the other?

A: "Want to go for a dip?"

Q: What do you get when you cross an ice cube with a dollar bill?

A: Cold cash.

Q: Did you hear about the woman who lost her job in the tuna factory?

A: She was canned.

Q: What kind of trousers do guitar players wear?

A: Chord-uroys.

Q: What do you get when you cross Jack Frost with Dracula?

A: Frostbite.

Q: What's the best day to eat ice cream?

A: Sundae.

Q: What do you get when you cross corn with a snowstorm?

A: Cornflakes.

Q: If bread had feet, what kind of shoes would it wear?

A: Loafers.

Q: What's a coward's favorite food?

A: Chicken!

Q: What kind of fruit do you find on ships?

A: Naval oranges.

Q: Did you hear about the man who lost his job in the bubble gum factory?

A: He bit off more than he could chew.

Q: What day is the best day to drink milk?

A: Thirst-day.

Q: What is a monster's favorite dessert?

A: Ice scream.

Q: Did you hear about the woman who lost her job in the orange juice factory?

A: She couldn't concentrate.

Q: What do presidents eat during elections?

A: Candied-dates.

Q: Did you hear about the man who lost his job growing beans?

A: He stalked out.

Q: Why did the fish jump out of the tanning bed?

A: It didn't want to get fried.

Q: Why is a baker never rich?

A: Because he always kneads dough!

Q: Why didn't Mom go the concert?

A: Because all they played was Pop music.

Q: Did you hear about the woman who lost her job in the potato factory?

A: She got sacked.

Q: Have you heard of a group called the Fishermen?

A: They aren't that bad, but they're always out of tuna.

Q: What do you get when you cross the Milky Way with a zebra?

A: The Stars and Stripes.

Q: Why don't plumbers like coffeemakers?

A: They don't like to see all those drips.

Q: What do you get when you cross a genie with a skeleton?

A: Wishbones.

Q: How does a candidate catch trout?

A: With a fishing poll.

Q: What did the mayonnaise say to the refrigerator?

A: "Close the door. I'm dressing!"

Q: Why did the computer walk with a cane?

A: Because it had a slipped disk.

Q: What presidential vacuum cleaner is displayed in the Smithsonian Institution?

A: Herbert's Hoover.

Q: Why was the guitar so sad?

A: Because everybody was always picking on him.

Q: Why did the amplifier take speech lessons?

A: It wanted to be a better speaker.

Q: What do you get when you cross a mountaintop with a ghost?

A: A peak-a-boo.

Q: Did you hear about the woman who lost her job doing bird imitations?

A: She didn't give a hoot.

Q: What did Shakespeare write about a sad president?

A: "Harding is such sweet sorrow. . . . "

Q: What do you get when you cross a parrot with a clock?

A: A bird that ticks when it talks.

Q: Did you hear about the man who lost his job as a fisher?

A: He floundered.

Q: How do presidents make old-fashioned candy in the White House?

A: They have a Taft-y pull.

Q: Why was the electric razor so nervous?

A: It had a close shave.

Q: How did the blind man know he was in the White House flower garden?

A: By the Theodore Rose-he-felt.

Q: Did you hear about the woman who lost her job as a shoemaker?

A: She got the boot.

Q: What spice does a president use?

A: Ronald's O-Reagan-o.

Q: What do you get when you cross a clock with a belt?

A: A waist of time.

Q: Why did the fisherman go to the trout stream on Election Day?

A: To "cast" his ballot.

Q: What do you get when you cross a Chevrolet with a radio?

A: Cartunes.

Q: What weapons will presidents use in outer space?

A: Ray-guns.

Q: Why was the iron in such a big hurry?

A: It was pressed for time.

Q: How do you know when a turkey is full?

A: When it's stuffed!

Q: What do you get when you cross a camel with a garbage truck?

A: Humpty Dumpty.

Q: What happened after the two TV sets got married?

A: They had a nice reception.

Q: What do you get when you cross a wizard with a UFO?

A: A flying sorceror.

Q: What do you get when you cross a dollar bill with a track star?

A: A fast buck.

Q: Did you hear about the man who lost his job as a peace activist?

A: He protested.

Q: What do you get when you cross Dracula with your teacher?

A: A blood test.

Q: Why did the two magnets fall in love?

A: Because they were attracted to each other.

Q: Did you hear about the woman who lost her job as a bookkeeper?

A: She couldn't keep her balance.

Q: What do you get when you cross your head with the kitchen sink?

A: A brain drain.

This book is available in two editions:
Library binding by Carolrhoda Books, Inc.,
   a division of Lerner Publishing Group
Soft cover by First Avenue Editions,
   an imprint of Lerner Publishing Group
241 First Avenue North
Minneapolis, MN 55401 U.S.A.

Website address: www.carolrhodabooks.com

Library of Congress Cataloging-in-Publication Data

   Let the fun begin : wacky what-do-you-get jokes, playful puns, and more / by
Scott K. Peterson . . . [et al.] ; pictures by Brian Gable.
      p.   cm. — (Make me laugh!)
Summary: Presents a variety of jokes, riddles, and puns.
   ISBN: 1−57505−661−5 (lib. bdg. : alk. paper)
   ISBN: 1−57505−738−7 (pbk. : alk. paper)
   1. Knock-knock jokes. 2. Wit and humor, Juvenile. [1. Knock-knock jokes.
2. Jokes. 3. Puns and punning. 4. Riddles.] I. Peterson, Scott K. II. Gable, Brian,
1949– ill. III. Series.
PN6231.K55L395 2005
818'.60208—dc22   2003019246

Manufactured in the United States of America
1 2 3 4 5 6 − DP − 10 09 08 07 06 05